THE WARTIME GARDEN

GARDEN

Twigs Way

Published in Great Britain in 2015 by Shire Publications Ltd, PO Box 883, Oxford, OX1 9PL, UK.

PO Box 3985, New York, NY 10185-3985, USA.

E-mail: shire@shirebooks.co.uk
www.shirebooks.co.uk

Shire Library no. 824.   ISBN-13: 978 1 78442 008 6
PDF e-book ISBN: 978 1 78442 052 9
ePub ISBN: 978 1 78442 051 2

Twigs Way has asserted her right under the Copyright, Designs and Patents Act, 1988, to be identified as the author of this book.

Typeset in Garamond Pro and Gill Sans.

Printed in China through Worldprint Ltd.

15 16 17 18 19   10 9 8 7 6 5 4 3 2 1

COVER IMAGE
Front cover design by Peter Ashley; 'Dig for Victory' poster, collection of Mike Brown. Back cover: detail from a Second World War poster.

TITLE PAGE IMAGE
Detail from image on page 31.

CONTENTS PAGE IMAGE
With part of the flower borders being taken up by vegetables, any decorative plants were often crammed into small spaces.

ACKNOWLEDGMENTS
I would like to thank Ursula Buchan (author of *A Green and Pleasant Land*), Mike Brown (specialist in the Second World War and the Home Front) and Philip Norman of the Garden Museum for their help and advice.

I would also like to thank the people who have allowed me to use illustrations which are acknowledged as follows:

Alamy, page 22 (Image no. C8F4M2); Mike Brown pages 12 (bottom), 13 (right), 14, 18, 20, 21, 25, 31 (both), 34, 38, 39 (bottom), 40 (bottom), 45, 48, 54, 55; Ideal Home, pages 3, 30 (right); Imperial War Museum pages 17 (Image D8336), 29 left (Image PST3448), 37 (Image D17524); Estate of Abram Games, page 26; The Garden Museum pages 4, 6 (left), 10, 13 (left), 15, 24, 28, 43 (bottom), 46 (top), 50, 51, 52, 56, 62.

Shire Publications is supporting the Woodland Trust, the UK's leading woodland conservation charity, by funding the dedication of trees.

CONTENTS

By Helping Yourself You Help the Nation

WAR-TIME GARDENING

for Home Needs

CONTENTS

Feeding the Family
Essential Tools.
Work to Plan.
Making a Start.
Digging and
Trenching.
Sowing and
Planting.
Cropping for
Profit.
Crop Rotation.
Manuring.
Bottling and
Storing.
    Etc., Etc.

CONTENTS

Vegetables of
Many Kinds and
their Cultivation
including :—
Root and
Green Crops.
Salads.
Herbs.
Tomatoes.
Profitable Small
Fruits.
Crops for the
Greenhouse.
Cold Frames.
    Etc., Etc.

A NATIONAL FOOD HANDBOOK
issued by

Amateur Gardening

THE NATIONAL GARDEN WEEKLY

FULLY ILLUSTRATED

INTRODUCTION: 'THIS IS A FOOD WAR'

INSPIRING OVER 1.5 million allotments, 10 million leaflets and thousands of 'Victory Garden' fetes, 'Dig for Victory' was one of the most memorable and successful campaigns of the Second World War. The campaign defined the wartime garden: turning lawns into vegetable plots, flower borders to lettuce beds, and decorating Anderson air-raid shelters with marrows. Between the autumn of 1939 and the summer of 1945 the government variously enticed, cajoled and threatened the nation to take up forks and spades and do their bit on the 'Garden Front'. The gardens of Britain were its 'Line of Defence'. It was a line that looked to women and children, as well as to men, for support: bringing together town and country, rich and poor, to feed wartime Britain from its own vegetable gardens and maintain morale from its flower beds.

As an island nation, Great Britain had always been vulnerable to attack and blockade by sea and it was not until after the mid-twentieth century that substantial quantities of food were imported by air. The Napoleonic Wars (1803–15) forced increased home food production, expanded arable farming and raised food prices, leading in turn to civil unrest in 1815–20. In February 1915, just a few months into the First World War (1914–18), Kaiser Wilhelm II announced that both merchant and naval shipping in the waters around Great Britain would be destroyed without warning. The threat was renounced in 1916, but in February

Providing for the Home Front, the wartime garden played an essential role in victory.

OUT FOR VICTORY.

THE ALLOTMENT HOLDER.
Too old to fight, but doing his bit to beat the U boats.

The Gardens of Britain are A LINE OF DEFENCE
Gardener Wise says— GROW ALL THE FOOD YOU CAN

Above: The First World War had seen a Victory campaign on allotments and gardens.

Above right: Britain had always looked to its gardeners to overcome the impact of war and blockades.

1917 unrestrained U-boat warfare was reintroduced, with the aim of starving Britain into defeat. The response was a 'Victory' campaign that included the creation of over a million allotments, and exhortations that those too old to serve at the front should 'do their bit to beat the U-boats' in Britain's fields and gardens. In 1917 Britain's leaders had been unprepared for the impact of the German blockades and food shortages were a serious threat, especially as rationing was not put in place until 1918. Aptly, 1918 was the same year that Winston Churchill told to the poet and soldier Siegfried Sassoon that 'War is the normal occupation of man – war and gardening', when the two crossed swords in parliament.

By 1938, when the possibility of a Second World War became a probability, the nation was even more vulnerable to blockades than in 1917. Population growth, combined with the expansion of the suburbs and a move away from a food-producing economy, brought heavy reliance on food imports. In 1938 over 55 millions tons of food were imported by merchant shipping, including many of the items traditionally regarded as essential to the national diet. Ninety per cent of onions came from mainland Europe, fruit came from South Africa and Australia, bread wheat from Canada and the United States, tomatoes were imported from the Netherlands or the Channel Islands, and even apples were brought from France, leaving the orchards of Kent increasingly neglected. Numbers of allotments had dropped dramatically after the end of the First World War, and, although some 1930s suburban houses had been created with gardens of an equivalent size to an allotment, many urban families were

In my garden . . .

Looking back, it's difficult to visualise the garden as it used to be: the lawn that was just turning into a respectable bit of turf; the herbaceous border that made a glory of the summer months. Today the lawn is green only in memory but at least the vegetables which have taken its place don't need rolling and mowing: just a good foundation of FISONS GRANULAR VEGERITE to give them a healthy start. The glories of the pre-war herbaceous border faded long ago, but tomatoes, fed by FISONS 'TOMORITE' into bright and luscious ripeness, are a nearer and equally colourful memory, and a soft fruit crop raised on FISONS ICHTHEMIC GUANO can be as satisfying a sight, in its way, as the roses it replaced. One thing at least remains unchanged in peace or war: treat the earth generously and it will give back good measure. FISONS IMPROVED HOP MANURE provides humus and feeds, and FISONS CANARY GUANO is a general fertilizer, specially successful on light soils. (*Memo:* Must get in an order for a further supply of FISONS GROWMORE.)

It's Fisons for Fertilizers

 From Seedsmen and Stores. *In case of difficulty, kindly send name and address of your most convenient retailer to* FISONS Limited, (*Horticultural Department*), Harvest House, Ipswich. Largest makers of Complete Fertilizers. Pioneers of Granular Fertilizers.

housed in cramped high-density housing and tenements. In 1939 a population of 45 million shared only 3.5 million private gardens. With an expectation that merchant shipping would again be the subject of blockade, the Ministry of Agriculture and Fisheries calculated that, in such an emergency, private gardens and allotments could be made to produce a quarter of the nation's non-cereal foodstuffs. But getting the nation to feed itself would necessitate far-reaching change.

Between 1939 and 1945 war transformed the nation's gardens.

In the spring and summer of 1939 a small committee, its members drawn from the Royal Horticultural Society, the Ministry of Agriculture and Fisheries and the National Allotments Society, worked behind the scenes to produce the first strike from the Garden Front. Priced at 3d, *Food from the Garden* (Growmore Bulletin No. 1) aimed to inspire and inform the nation's gardeners on the outbreak of war: its publication on 9 September 1939 put the gardens of Great Britain on a wartime footing. As the *Gardeners' Chronicle* declared in its first edition after the outbreak of war (coincidentally also 9 September): 'Everybody whose whole time is not engaged in other forms of national defence, and

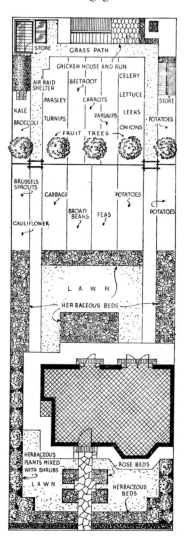

Left: A typical 1930s garden adapted to wartime conditions, with the lawn under vegetables. Taken from Richard Suddell's *Practical Gardening and Food Production*, published in 1940.

Above right: Home food production would play a vital role in winning the war by replacing food imports, as this advertisement explained.

Below right: In wartime, there was no space for cargoes of food if it could be grown at home instead.

who has a garden or garden plot or allotment, can render good service to the community by cultivating it to the fullest possible extent.'

FOOD
FROM
THE GARDEN

GROWMORE BULLETIN NO. I OF THE
MINISTRY OF AGRICULTURE AND FISHERIES

PUBLISHED BY
HIS MAJESTY'S STATIONERY OFFICE   PRICE 3d NET

Food from the Garden was the first Growmore bulletin. Although largely superseded by shorter, free leaflets, there were two further bulletins aimed at the home gardener, on preserving foods, and pests and diseases.

"Dig for Victory"

"Let this be the slogan of every one with a garden : of every able-bodied man and woman capable of digging an allotment in their spare time.

"In war we must make every effort. All the potatoes, all the cabbages, and all the other vegetables, we can produce may be needed. That is why I appeal to you, lovers of this great country of ours, to dig, to cultivate, to sow, and to plant.

"Our fellow-countrymen in the Forces abroad and at home are playing their part. I am confident that you, equally, will do yours by producing the maximum food from gardens and allotments."

R. H. Dorman Smith

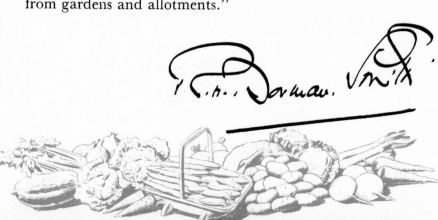

GETTING DUG IN

In October 1939 *Garden Work for Amateurs* enthusiastically reported that 'throughout the country gardens were a hive of activity', 'extending their existing kitchen garden portion of the garden by taking in all or part of the lawn'. However, such enthusiasm among the gardening press and public quickly wore off as the anticipated air raids and gas attacks failed to materialise in the months that would become known as 'the bore war'. When the Minister for Agriculture, Sir Reginald Dorman-Smith, announced the creation of 500,000 new allotment plots in public parks in the autumn of 1939, take-up was disappointing. The winter of 1939–40, the worst for fifty years, was not kind to those gardeners who did respond to the government's initial call to the Garden Front, and by spring the 'Grow More' campaign had failed to grow as much as the government had hoped. Alarmed by the slow response, the government relaunched the campaign, adopting the new slogan of 'Dig for Victory', accompanied by the 'foot and spade' that was to become the campaign's instantly recognisable symbol. Variously claimed as the 'live-action' foot of Mr McKie of Acton (a popular allotment site for the official war photographers' publicity shots) or a staged image, the boot-clad foot encapsulated the gritty new determination of the campaign.

Coinciding with the first food shortages and rationing, the new campaign stirred the nation's gardeners into action. Drafting in the businessman, politician, and excellent

A direct appeal to every man and woman to serve on the Garden Front.

Above: The new 'Dig for Victory' slogan was officially launched in the spring of 1940 but had been used by advertisers since autumn 1939.

The foot that inspired a million new gardeners – but whose was it?

publicist Lord Woolton as Minister of Food in April of 1940 (until 1943), the government hoped to inspire the nation through its stomach. As Lord Woolton famously declared: 'This is a Food War. Every extra row of vegetables in allotments saves shipping. If we grow more Potatoes we need not import so much Wheat. Carrots and Swedes, which can be stored through the winter, help to replace imported fruit ... The battle on the Kitchen Front cannot be won without help from the Kitchen Garden.' In response, novice gardeners dug up their lawns, emptied their flower beds and got ready for (vegetable) planting. 'What to plant?' was answered by the government in the first of its new series of Dig for Victory leaflets. Concerned that gardeners would favour the quick and easy delights of lettuces, peas, radishes and tomatoes, they sternly emphasised what became known as 'the Vegetables of National Importance': parsnips, carrots, and potatoes – important sources of carbohydrate and sugars that could be kept in store through the autumn and winter – accompanied by kale, cabbage, sprouts and leeks for vitamins and iron through the winter and spring months.

Seeds were obtained, often at reduced price, through allotment societies and garden clubs, as well as direct from seed merchants or from Woolworths – who sold Cuthbert's seeds. There was no national 'rationing' of retail seed supplies, so shortages were frequent, and the situation was not improved by the inclusion of lists of recommended varieties in the numerous Dig for Victory bulletins – each in

Grow for Winter as well as Summer

DIG FOR VICTORY LEAFLET No.1.   New Series

Vegetables for you and your family every week of the year. Never a week without food from your garden or allotment. Not only fresh peas and lettuce in June— new potatoes in July, but all the health-giving vegetables in WINTER — when supplies are scarce - - - — SAVOYS, SPROUTS, KALE, SPROUTING BROCCOLI, ONIONS, LEEKS, CARROTS, PARSNIPS and BEET

Vegetables all the year round if you

DIG WELL AND CROP WISELY

Follow this Plan

ISSUED BY THE MINISTRY OF AGRICULTURE

turn causing a rush on supplies. The Ministry of Agriculture responded with the Dig for Victory leaflet *Saving Your Own Seeds*, and gardeners were expected to club together to save and share seed or, even better, seedlings. An ounce of leek seed could produce enough young plants to go round several allotment plots if the thinnings were redistributed rather than thrown away as would have been done in peacetime. Seed was also sent from the United States direct to the National Allotments Society. Ninety tons had been sent this way by January 1943 – much of it with personal messages of encouragement from individual donors. Local donations were made from large country-house gardens: at Gatton Park, Surrey, Josiah Coleman raised twenty thousand seedling plants under glass for donation to local smallholders. Tools could be obtained through allotment and garden clubs, with the guidelines of one wheelbarrow

Above left: Vegetables competed with the air-raid shelter for space in the garden.

Above: Promising crops throughout the year, Dig for Victory Leaflet No. I reflected the government's very real concern of winter starvation. The use of colour was abandoned for later leaflets.

between five plots, although, as metal became increasingly scarce, new tools were hard to come by.

To assist novice gardeners, Dig for Victory Leaflet No. 20 was entitled *How to Dig*, rather oddly following No. 19, *How to Sow Seed* (physically the smallest, being the size of a seed packet). There were eventually to be twenty-six Dig for Victory leaflets, covering everything from planning your crops, digging, sowing, dealing with pests and diseases, storing (how to make clamps and drying racks), and making preserves. Early numbers also dealt with individual crops

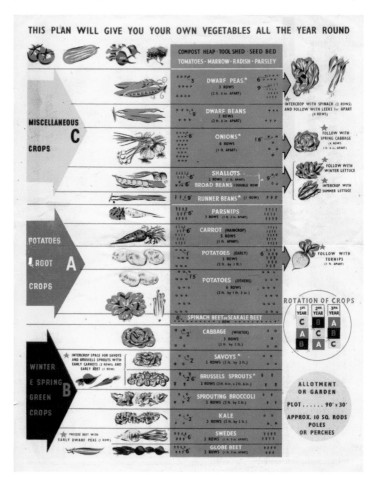

The plan in Dig for Victory Leaflet No. 1. The small area for potatoes reflected the government's initial belief that farmers would be able to provide all the potatoes needed.

such as potatoes, onions, leeks, shallots, peas, beans, cabbages and root crops. Once published, the leaflets were regularly updated to take account of the latest food or seed shortages, and the Ministry of Agriculture kept track of how many copies of each leaflet had been printed and distributed. The most popular were leaflet No. 8 on tomato growing, and those on planning 10-pole and 5-pole plots (leaflets 1 and 23). The leaflets were still being issued as late as 1944 (No. 24 *Roof and Window Box Gardening*, No. 25 *How to Prune Fruit Trees and Bushes*, and No. 26 *How to Use Cloches*).

Leaflet No. 7 *Manure from Garden Rubbish* addressed a problem that had become apparent early on in the war, namely reduced availability of organic manures and fertilisers. In 1942 the 'radio gardener' Cecil Middleton recommended 'a few buckets' of fresh horse manure for the growing of mushrooms, but added that, although it was easy enough to get hold of in the countryside, one would have to 'watch your opportunities' in the town. Stable manure became almost impossible to get, especially for town dwellers, with prices soaring to 12s a load. Manures based on hops were widely used in the first years of the war, having the advantage of being clean to handle and relatively odour-free. As J. R. Wade remarked in his book *War-Time Gardening*, a large bag of

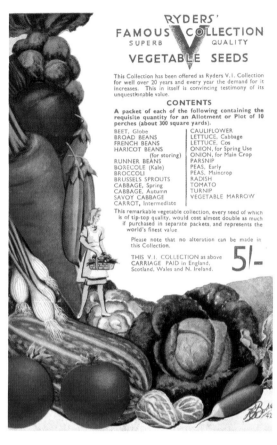

In response to the recommended planting plans, several seed companies sold special collections comprising all that was needed for one's plot.

MANURES
FOR THE WAR-TIME GARDEN
S. B. WHITEHEAD, D.Sc.

A Guide for the Conversion of
Garden and Household Refuse into Plant Food

A NATIONAL FOOD HANDBOOK
ISSUED BY "AMATEUR GARDENING"

Manures and fertilisers were in short supply, and substitutes included everything from hair to street sweepings. Compost heaps were new to many gardeners, and a leaflet was available on how to create them.

hop manure – costing 7s – could replace 15 hundredweight of stable manure. Popular varieties were 'Abel', 'Adcompost' and 'Wakeley's'. Swanley Horticultural College used 'London dung', which arrived by lorry and was said to have 'a peculiar smell and included old pieces of corset and a lot of paper'. Seaweed, 'night soil' (human manure), sludge from sewage treatment plants, shoddy (clippings from the wool-cloth industry), street sweepings, ash and soot from the numerous domestic fires, and hair collected and bagged from hair salons were among other solutions. In 1942 the government introduced 'National Growmore' fertiliser to compensate for shortages of traditional sources of gardener's potash (imported pre-war from Russia and Spain) and nitrogen (traditionally from guano sources in the Canary Islands). 'National Growmore' (or '7,7,7' as it also became known) contained 7 per cent nitrogen, 7 per cent potassium and 7 per cent phosphorus, and was available for allotment holders and vegetable gardeners, although in 1945 it too came under ration.

Garden Work for Amateurs carried weekly news from allotments across the country as the wartime garden took on a public face. High-profile sites such as the Tower of London moat (surely the best fertilised soil ever used for an allotment site) and Kensington Gardens gained media prominence. The Bethnal Green Bombed Sites Producers' Association hosted the Duke of Norfolk in 1941 and then the Queen in 1943. On the latter visit a goat ate the Dig for Victory leaflets in the Queen's hands. Princess Elizabeth and Princess Margaret were later photographed studying their own Dig for Victory leaflets in the rather safer environs of

Most urban parks, including the Royal Parks in London (Kensington Gardens is shown here), had substantial areas of allotments.

Buckingham Palace. An additional fillip to the campaign in the form of a further 500,000 allotments was announced in autumn 1940, and ambitious plans were made for one allotment for every five households, an average that was eventually exceeded in towns in endangered areas. Sittingbourne (Kent) had two thousand plots for five thousand households by spring 1945, while Thetford (Norfolk) had one for every two households. Away from the south-east, Newcastle had five thousand allotments by 1941, Cardiff over three thousand, and Kettering two thousand, while Sheffield (at heart a working-class manufacturing city) had an estimated nine thousand plots.

PRESERVES FROM THE GARDEN

"GROWMORE" BULLETIN No. 3
OF THE MINISTRY OF AGRICULTURE
AND FISHERIES PUBLISHED BY
HIS MAJESTY'S STATIONERY OFFICE
PRICE 4d. NET

ALL HANDS TO THE FORK

'START DIGGING NOW – women and older children as well as men' was the message in government advertisements by 1941 as concern grew that Home Guard and Air Raid Precautions (ARP) duties (as well as active service) distracted men from the vegetable garden and that insufficient women were replacing them. Previously, women had been largely relegated to the role of cook for the vegetables and fruits the men were growing, but now the government swung into action with a range of propaganda posters and leaflets that showed women in action on the Garden Front. Dig for Victory Leaflet No. 19, *How to Sow Seeds*, had a woman on the front cover, sensibly dressed in low shoes and tweed jacket. *Garden Work for Amateurs* reported on inspiring success stories, such as an (unnamed) Cornish woman who worked eight hours a day in a factory, had two children, a husband away in the services, and still kept a brood of hens and produced 100 pounds of onions, 1,500 leeks and 7 hundredweight of potatoes from her allotments.

A series of newspaper advertisements showed men instructing women in digging and other garden tasks, all directed at those 'thousands who will be growing their own vegetables for the first time'. 'Remember,' claimed one such advertisement, 'many Victory Diggers have had very little experience and that many more must now be women. They will be glad of your tips and help.' However, many of the women who ventured on to the allotments for the first time

Traditionally the role played by women was in the kitchen rather than the garden.

HOW TO SOW SEEDS

DIG FOR VICTORY LEAFLET
NUMBER 19   (NEW SERIES)

ISSUED BY THE MINISTRY OF AGRICULTURE

The appearance of a woman on the front of this Dig for Victory leaflet marked a distinct change in the government's approach to the contribution women would make on the Home and Garden Front.

had more than enough 'tips and help' from men who were not as anxious as the Ministry of Agriculture to have women invading the plots. Mrs Cope Morgan (subject of a BBC Overseas broadcast) recalled that, when she and her daughter took a plot, 'advice was showered on us, for we were the only WOMEN [plot] holders'. Having lived in West Africa for many years, Mrs Cope Morgan could keep her end up, as she said, but other women felt weighed down with the constant advice and criticism, and, despite the establishment in Preston of the first ever Women Allotments Holders' and Gardeners' Association in June 1942, a government survey in the autumn of that year revealed a disappointing 183 female respondents to a survey of three thousand allotment holders – and no more women could be found to include in the survey. Entries for the Certificate of Merit Scheme for allotment gardens revealed a similarly low proportion of female applicants — only 1 per cent of the total in the Bridgwater area, for example.

Reasons for this poor take-up can be surmised from the editorials and advertisements in women's magazines of the period. On the plus side, gardening was claimed to keep you fit, improve your figure and entertain the children, as well as providing valuable foodstuffs with the newly prominent vitamins for the family table. On the minus side, seen obliquely through the letters pages and advertisements, nail polish would be chipped, hands coarsened, backs put out, and clothes ruined. *Gardening Made Easy* admitted that 'gardening is hard on clothes and really presentable ones should never be worn for it'. Many must have empathised with the women described by Mrs R. Hudson (wife of the then Minister of Agriculture): 'fighting a lone battle in their gardens and plots against insects and weather; they are often disappointed and very tired.'

Ryders'
SEEDS
FOR BEST RESULTS
1941

SOW FOR VICTORY

RYDER & SON (1920) LTD. S⁺ ALBANS, ENGLAND

Ryders, the seed merchants, appear to have taken their lead from the Ministry of Agriculture in their 1941 advertising.

Film actress Ann Todd was recruited to the campaign to get more women in the vegetable garden. Her immaculate hair and dress were a far cry from the gardening appearance of most women.

For women left to run households and families on their own, the vegetable plot was a place where children could usefully tire themselves out, while hopefully contributing to their own dinner. Even the younger members of the family could be set to weeding, picking off caterpillars and other pests, or occasionally harvesting small and fiddly crops such as peas, while older children gained experience and training as part of the Dig for Victory school gardens campaign.

The scale of production of school gardens could be substantial. In the West Riding of Yorkshire, the *Gardeners' Chronicle* reported 400 acres were cultivated by twenty thousand children. In Knighton-on-Teme (Worcestershire)

130 meals a day were produced for the schoolchildren from gardens they tended themselves, while Westcliff High School (Essex) grew 2 hundredweight each of carrots, parsnips, beetroot and runner beans in their first year at their evacuation site, with enlarged grounds being taken on the following year. The Maisemore School Club (Gloucestershire) supplemented the produce from its quarter of an acre garden with pigs, poultry, rabbits and even bees. In 1943 they produced fifty thousand eggs as well as 8 tons of bacon and 5 hundredweight of honey!

IRIS MARSHALL.
THE GARDENER.

Gardening not only fed the family but kept children occupied.

Postcards of the period reflected the importance of the Garden Front, including this charming example of a young woman grappling with an enormous cabbage. The sender added in the name of the recipient (her aunt).

BROADCASTS TO   SCHOOLS

SCIENCE

AND

GARDENING

SPRING TERM 1938   PRICE 2d.

In 1938 school radio broadcasts had included a series called 'Science and Gardening', and this proved invaluable as a starting point for digging for victory.

In schools with many evacuees, school gardens or allotments performed a dual function of helping to feed the influx and providing occupation for the children when it was their turn to vacate the classrooms. Schools with limited accommodation ran lessons for evacuees on alternate days or using morning/afternoon shifts, and the outdoor activities of gardening and collecting rosehips (for vitamin-rich syrups) or wild fruits occupied those not in lessons. Rivalry was often intense because each class would be given an allotment or garden area of its own.

In London and other cities that had sustained heavy bombing boys clubs and brigades in particular were active in establishing allotments and community farms in the ruins. The Ministry of Information recorded the work of Webbe Boys' Club in East London, where boys of ten and eleven years old were creating allotments on a bomb site, in readiness for planting beans and other vegetables sent from the United States. In the same year the Girls' Training Corps were shown learning to dig and sow on an 'allotment' created in the gardens of 145 Piccadilly, the former home of the King and Queen, but now a bomb site. These bomb-site gardens lasted into the post-war period, and in the autumn of 1945 Pathé News recorded one of the most productive of children's allotment sites in the heart of London, under the title *How Does Your Garden Grow*.

Concerned at the continued shortage of onions both at home and for the armed forces, the Horticultural Committee of the Red Cross came up with the idea of Onion Clubs, where groups of twelve to twenty members would grow onions to sell direct to nearby Navy, Army and Air Force

Institutes (NAAFIs), or to contractors for the Admiralty, who would arrange collection and distribution. The onions would feed the forces and the funds would be donated to the Red Cross. The National Allotments Society weighed in with certificates and prizes for its members who took part, but the scheme was taken up with particular enthusiasm by schools. At Walpole Highway, Wisbech (Cambridgeshire), schoolchildren raised almost 200 pounds of onions for the scheme, sold at the agreed price of £25 a ton, to be paid direct to the Red Cross. Onions were perhaps a safe crop for children to grow, as the raw onion held no temptations for 'snacking' while gardening. Fresh peas and fruits were rather more tempting – the government urged parents to offer chilled carrots on a stick as a substitute for ice cream!

Southwark evacuees helping to grow their own dinners.

GROW YOUR OWN FOOD
supply your own cookhouse

GETTING THE MESSAGE OUT

Poster campaigns played an important role in all areas of the Home Front during the war, and the wartime garden was no exception. As well as the 'trademark' foot on the spade that relaunched the campaign, artists were commissioned to produce designs for colourful, high-quality images. Mary Tunbridge won a competition with her poster of a child carrying hoe and spade, although the markedly cracked and dry ground underfoot does not encourage thoughts of gardening. 'For Their Sake Grow Your Own Vegetables', depicting the spade and foot, but with the smiling faces of young children in the background, made a direct and somewhat dramatic appeal to parents to provide for their family. Abram Games was employed by the War Office between 1941 and 1946, producing over a hundred poster designs. Among these were the visually playful 'Use Spades not Ships' and the plot to table image with the slogan 'Every Piece of Land must be Cultivated'. Both also carried the caption 'Grow Your Own Food and Supply Your Own Cookhouse', aimed at forces billeted in country houses and rural areas. Overlapping with the messages from the Ministry of Agriculture and the War Office were the posters backed by the Ministry of Food, emphasising the nutritional values of foodstuffs such as potatoes and carrots.

With newspapers from *The Times* to the *Daily Express* carrying their own gardening columns (and in many cases, publishing associated gardening books), advice was

Visually playful, this Abram Games poster made the connection between plot and plate.

never far away, although *The Times* was intermittent in its contributions and did not lend its support to its garden columnists' publication *A Garden Goes to War*. The *Daily Mail*'s Percy Izzard (author of *Food from the Garden in War-Time*) vied with E. T. Brown of the *Daily Express* (*Make Your Garden Feed You*) and *Amateur Gardening* magazine's *War-Time Gardening for Home Needs,* while W. E. Shewell, an early proponent of organic and 'no dig' gardening, brought out *Grow Your Own Food Supply*. Shewell was able to enlist the aid of his wife, Irene, for an accompanying work on *Cook What You Grow*. *Garden Work for Amateurs* ran weekly reports on numbers of allotments, weight of crops grown, and notable achievements of the numerous Victory and Red Cross shows. Towns competed against each other for recognition of their achievements, with council representatives and allotment associations sending reports to local and national newspapers as well as back to the government. Advice columns in those same periodicals and papers dealt with a range of queries, from the difference between superphosphate and superphosphate of lime (none), to the growing of tomatoes in flower borders (only if in full sun), and whether one could grow your own sugar beet (yes, but it would not be usable as sugar). It must have come as a relief for these hard-pressed editors to turn to the perennial correspondence on potting up lily of the valley, and recommending flowers for shady areas, among the more challenging wartime demands. Other popular periodicals aimed at the wartime

In the first years of the war, seed catalogues had colour covers, making them media propaganda in their own right.

Ryders'

"GROW MORE FOOD"

SEEDS FOR RESULTS
1940

gardener included *Home Gardening* and the *Gardeners' Chronicle* – the latter usually the choice of the more dedicated or working gardener but widening its readership in the war years. *Ideal Home* also widened its coverage to include food production and became *Ideal Home and Gardening.* Not widening its readership was the upmarket *My Garden: An Intimate Magazine for Garden Lovers,* whose pages gave little practical support for those grappling with weedy allotments or wilting onions, focusing instead on difficulties caused to its readers by the conscription of their gardeners, the difficulties in maintaining a tennis lawn, or the shortage of flower stocks in plant nurseries.

With 3.5 million listeners for its Sunday lunchtime slot, *In Your Garden* with Cecil Middleton (widely known as 'Mr Middleton') was the most popular of the radio garden shows, and the government used him to help 'get over the stuff we shall be putting out for the guidance of gardeners'.

Left: If you were not inspired to Dig for Victory, then digging for health might tempt you into the garden.

Right: Almost every newspaper had its own garden writer, each of whom launched a wartime garden book.

Left: Gardeners had a wide choice of books to guide them, although all books were soon restricted to 'wartime economy' paper and print, with only line drawings for illustration. Several combined gardening and cooking.

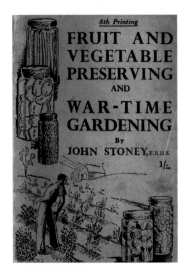

Right: In addition to its usual coverage of interiors and flower borders, *Ideal Home* ran articles on home food production and smallholdings, changing its name to *Ideal Home and Gardening*.

Mr Middleton's personal style struck the right note of encouragement for those struggling to fit in gardening among other duties, combined with sympathy for things gone wrong or left undone. In 1942 the BBC launched *Radio Allotment*. Recorded on location from an allotment in West London, the presenters – Wynford Vaughan-Thomas, Raymond Glendenning, and Stewart MacPhearson – talked through their weekly tasks, although a *Radio Times* cartoon suggested that at least some of the work was carried out by a support team of women. Gardening also appeared on *The Brains Trust* (from 1942 onwards), which led to local gardening *Brains Trust* events. Also reaching the local audience were the five instructional gardening films produced by Plant Protection Ltd under the aegis of the government. These were shown at Home Guard meetings, in communal air-raid shelters, and anywhere else a 'captive' audience was guaranteed.

Playing on the theme of garden plot to table top, a Pathé newsreel was used to warn people of the importance of planning for winter crops. The short film opened with a man sitting at a dining table doubling as a vegetable plot. A waiter

with your radio
dealer's help
you can listen to

'IN YOUR
GARDEN'

on your present set
for a long time
to come—consult him

A radio as good as Ferranti is worth holding on to at any time. And especially so in these days when the output of new sets is restricted.

make the most of your

FERRANTI
radio

MIDDLETON'S

ALL THE YEAR ROUND

GARDENING

GUIDE

"STEP BY STEP—WEEK BY WEEK THROUGH THE FOUR SEASONS"

2/6

Above: Instantly recognisable by his hat and glasses, and with a reassuring voice, Mr Middleton became *the* wartime media gardener. Despite becoming the voice of the Dig for Victory campaign, Mr Middleton's passion was flowers and it was said of him that 'he could not love an onion where a dahlia might grow'. Sadly he died in 1947, just when his beloved flowers were re-appearing in gardens everywhere.

Left: Radio was an essential source of information during the war, although new radios were soon difficult to obtain.

(a thinly disguised Father Time) watches over the scene as the man feasts on salads and summer foods, stepping forward to ask what he will order for his winter course. Heedless of the future, the 'diner' refuses to order and the final scene depicts snow enveloping the table/garden with no food or growth in sight; the unhappy diner sprawls across the frozen scene, desperate for something to eat. Father Time, now bearing

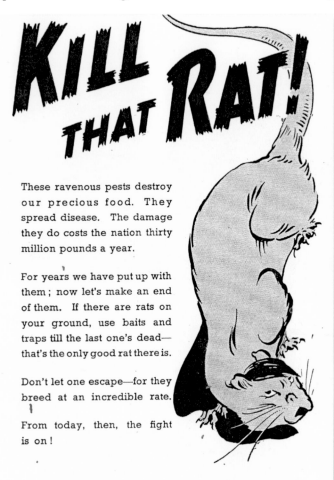

KILL THAT RAT!

These ravenous pests destroy our precious food. They spread disease. The damage they do costs the nation thirty million pounds a year.

For years we have put up with them; now let's make an end of them. If there are rats on your ground, use baits and traps till the last one's dead— that's the only good rat there is.

Don't let one escape—for they breed at an incredible rate.

From today, then, the fight is on!

Your County War Agricultural Executive Committee is eager to help you. Ask them for a copy of the special Leaflet on

Media campaigns took on a patriotic theme – pests were often depicted with German flags, or, as here, with Hitler's features.

lilies to lay across the corpse, adds a final commentary on the need to plan and plant ahead. As a companion piece to the rather more positive tones of *Grow for Winter as Well as Summer* (Dig for Victory Leaflet No. 1), this small piece of theatre is sobering and slightly surreal and perhaps reflects the seriousness of the food situation at its date of production (1943).

In a more jolly mood, a 1940 Pathé reel portrayed a blind allotment holder who had been awarded the Dig for Victory Diploma. He was filmed harvesting potatoes and beans on his Manchester allotment before barrowing the produce back home, and the jaunty commentary imparted an odd contrast to the serious mien of the gardener himself. This was one of several 'newsflash' reels aimed at persuading the disabled and the elderly to take up the Dig for Victory call, and to shame the able-bodied by example.

In 1944 Cecil Middleton provided the voice-over for two cartoons on wartime gardening – *Compost Heaps for Feeding Plants* and *Blitz on Bugs*. A 'plant canteen' featured in the first, with 'factory workers' changing compost heaps into steaming piles of food that were then delivered via 'train' to hungry plants. By 1944, many of the audience would have been very familiar with the inside of factory canteens and so the Disney-inspired cartoon would have struck a chord. The final shot reminds the audience that 'Ministry of Agriculture and Fisheries Dig for Victory Leaflet No. 7 (on compost heaps) tells you how'. *Blitz on Bugs* was also linked to the leaflet campaign with the motto 'Tackle the pest, tackle him early, Dig for Victory Leaflet No. 16, tells you how', while the bugs themselves are shown planning their plant invasion with military precision.

One message that did not get out during the war was the weather forecast. In order to hinder enemy manoeuvres, no forecasts were broadcast between 5 September 1939 and 2 April 1945, making gardening rather unpredictable!

GOLD FROM YOUR BACKYARD

With the Dig for Victory campaign in full swing, the nation's tables were theoretically groaning under the weight of home-produced vegetables, but, as *The Wartime Weekend Gardener* (1942) declared, 'The aim of the good gardener is to supply his household with as much fresh produce as possible', and this meant eggs and meat as well as vegetables. As wartime gardening books appended chapters on hutches, pens and piggeries, local councils temporarily revoked regulations banning the keeping of livestock in towns, and the 'Backyarders' came into existence.

Producing feathers, meat and even fertiliser as well as eggs (otherwise rationed at one a week), hens were the most popular back-garden livestock. In 1939 it was estimated there were already five million hens kept in gardens and backyards, a number that was to double in the war years. Initially demand for laying hens outstripped supply, competing as it was with demand for the eggs, and obtaining layers became difficult. By 1941 pullet (young female hen) stocks were restricted and a novice hen-keeper was only permitted feed for up to twelve birds. In practice most amateur hen-keepers limited themselves to half a dozen hens, with the cockerel optional – although his presence guaranteed future laying stock, as well as eventually making a satisfying Sunday dinner.

In his book *Practical Gardening and Food Production in Pictures*, Richard Suddell's plan, 'Your Garden Adapted for Wartime', recommended placing the hen house between

It was a fine line between wasting human food and giving scraps to hens and rabbits. Poultry rations were increased when it was discovered that many home flocks were performing badly.

For the Backyarder, vegetables were not enough, and gardening magazines competed with periodicals on smallholding and raising livestock.

the compost bed and the greenhouse, close to the air-raid shelter at the end of the garden. From here, he wrote, the chickens could be allowed to roam the orchard (notably lacking in the accompanying plan of a small suburban garden) but be restrained from the bush fruits and brassicas. Wire netting, essential for keeping rats from the coop, was inevitably in short supply, with even the domestic poultry keeper clubs running out despite their priority claim, and old tennis and football netting was pressed into service as a substitute.

Under wartime rules, no food 'fit for human consumption' could be discarded, and, depending on how harshly this was interpreted, this might include potato waste, stale bread and crusts, vegetable peelings, peas, beans, and even hedgerow berries, which were traditionally used to boost poultry health in winter. Seed was available for those who wanted to grow their own crops to feed livestock, typically including oats and corn as well as buckwheat, clover, dandelion and chives, but all of these took up space in an already crowded garden or allotment plot.

Many gardening books and magazines, even those aimed at suburban gardeners, started to run columns on keeping a range of livestock.

Balancer meal, a ready-made grain-based meal for hens, could be obtained through joining local domestic poultry

Home Food Production.   The Ideal Home and Gardening   September, 1940

LIVESTOCK in Your GARDEN

keepers' clubs, of which hundreds sprang up. Hen feed was rationed after 1941 and obtainable only by a complex system of giving up one's own 'hard shell' egg ration. Egg production was poor on the standard ration of 4 pounds of balancer meal per hen and in June 1943 the ration was increased to 5 pounds per hen, but even so egg production did not officially keep pace with the increase in hen keeping. Neighbours could also be encouraged to join in the scheme, giving up their egg ration for your hens in return for a share of the eggs. As G. Ryley-Scott enthusiastically declared in his 1941 *Produce Your Own Eggs*, 'The householder who supplies his own family, and other families in the vicinity as well, with eggs and thus cuts down the consumption of meat and fish, is performing a wartime service of no small magnitude.' Ryley-Scott even went as far as claiming that hens would make 'gold from your backyard' – a claim incidentally also made for compost.

Rabbit meat was never officially rationed, and country dwellers made considerable inroads into the wild rabbit population to supplement their rations, as well as taking excess to market; but by 1942 the government had placed a fixed

Mrs Brown and her daughter Peggy tending the wartime flock at Rowney Green, Worcestershire. After the introduction of egg rationing, keeping hens became increasingly popular.

price on wild rabbits sold through butchers, putting them out of the reach of most families. In John Hampshire's 1941 *The War-time Week-end Gardener*, he declared: 'The keeping of rabbits has passed out of the hobby stage and, in the last year or two, has blossomed forth into an important national service'. He added that 'readers who have never even considered the keeping of rabbits will be eager to make a start'.

Organised clubs were set up to supply bran to supplement green feed, weeds and waste, and in return club members agreed to sell a minimum of 50 per cent of their produce to government-approved buyers (usually local butchers). By 1943 there were three thousand registered rabbit clubs handing out advice, feed, and the occasional wire netting – although the indoor Morrison air-raid shelter was also popularly adapted as an outdoor rabbit run. *The War-time Week-end Gardener* recommended Rex or Flemish Giant rabbits – the former for their velvet fur and the latter for their size, with one buck to three does. The feed recommendations in the same book (including left-over rice pudding, potatoes and gristle) and the hutch sizes given were indicative more of wartime conditions than welfare considerations, although some rabbits undoubtedly crossed the line from 'livestock' to pet. Indeed, a hint of exasperation may be heard in the author's exhortation that 'Before they can be eaten they must be killed … and even very sensitive people do keep rabbits and do their own killing'. The two-page description of killing and skinning that followed was probably enough to put most amateurs off the whole idea, and many a 'Flopsy' and 'Thumper' outlived the war.

Despite the immaculately made hutches and runs in this image, the reality was often hastily tacked together tea boxes, with chicken wire in short supply.

HOW TO KEEP RABBITS

1/-

THIS BOOK TELLS YOU HOW YOU CAN JOIN IN THE GOVERNMENT SCHEME TO PRODUCE MORE DOMESTIC RABBIT MEAT, FURS AND WOOL FOR YOURSELF AND FOR THE NATION

PUBLISHED BY "FUR & FEATHER, IDLE, BRADFORD, YORKS.

Children were often left in charge of the hens and rabbits, making the inevitable mealtime appearance of their charges traumatic.

Bees were a more complicated undertaking for the novice, with a heavy outlay in hives and equipment, and not suitable for the smaller garden, but despite this a craze for beekeeping swept the nation, and areas of allotments were put aside for communal hives. Beekeepers could apply for extra sugar supplies to keep the hives over winter, but there was official concern that much of this precious ration did not make it as far as the hives, so the sugar destined for bees was dyed green. The resulting bright green honey was so alarming that the under-researched government measure was instantly dropped.

In the hands of the novice or soft-hearted rabbit keeper, things could rapidly get out of hand!

'For those who have little time to spare and sometimes feel harassed by the rush of these days, a pen of pigs, especially after they have enjoyed a meal of kitchen waste, presents a restful picture and an antidote to worry' – so declared *The Times* in December 1940. For those who did not possess a park or garden sufficiently

Honey made a satisfying – if sometimes hazardous – substitute for sugar.

BEES are so INTERESTING and PROFITABLE

. . . the latter especially iu war time. Now is the time to plan for their reception.

large to accommodate pigs in such repose (or at a suitable remove), the reality was somewhat messier and undoubtedly noisier. Within urban and suburban areas at least, pigs were on the whole less popular, and also much easier for the government to keep tabs on. The 1943 figure of five thousand registered clubs with 110,000 members and 120,000 pigs is likely to be more accurate than the official figures for home-produced eggs or rabbits. In these urban areas, piggeries were most commonly created on allotment sites and became a common sight even in the centre of London. Pig swill – mixed left-over foodstuff for boiling before feeding – was collected from bins provided by local councils, and it was estimated that over 10,000 tons of meat a year was produced through clubs using this and other collection schemes. London's most famous piggery was in Hyde Park, although the efforts of the dustmen in Tottenham, collecting and sorting edible waste from general refuse, led to the contents of the communal swill bins being known as 'Tottenham pudding'.

Overenthusiastic Backyarders left little room for vegetables.

'BACKS TO THE LAND' today at 1.15 brings you more expert advice on how to turn that backyard to the best account.

'WHAT ABOUT THE FLOWERS?'

'A QUESTION WHICH presents itself to the mind of every gardener is – what about the flower garden in wartime'? The answer according to the *Gardeners' Chronicle*, and much of the gardening press, was that flowers should be allowed to stay. 'Flowers can play a far more important part in our lives in war-time than you may at first imagine' said the Ryders' seed company catalogue in the spring of 1941, 'brightening our homes by providing colour and harmony … and stimulating and brightening our mental outlook too!' Even the act of tending and growing flowers was 'soothing on the nerves and mind in a time of stress and strain'. Keeping the flower garden in trim may not have rated as patriotic as vegetable growing, but where flowers did make an appearance their upkeep should not be neglected. As Cecil Middleton noted in his March 1942 talk, 'We haven't had much to say about the flowers lately. Obviously, in these times when food growing is all important, flowers must take a back seat, but it doesn't follow that we must neglect them altogether. If they have all been swept away to make room for more vegetables, then there is nothing more to be said about them, but if they are still there, occupying space, they might just as well be looked after and made the most of. An untidy, neglected flower border, overgrown with weeds and rubbish, is neither use nor ornament …'

Many seed suppliers were able to offer only an abridged list, usually the hardiest and most easily grown varieties,

As Victory Gardens flourished, finding space for the flowers required military planning!

vegetables versus flowers

HAVE YOU A PLAN OF CAMPAIGN?

Gardening periodicals, along with plant nurseries and seed merchants, had an interest in fighting for the role of flowers in the wartime garden.

GROW FOOD... BUT DON'T GIVE UP FLOWERS

Dig for victory—but don't neglect the cheerfulness and colour that the cultivation of flowers can bring to your home, especially during the dark days of war. Ensure success with the weekly aid of HOME GARDENING, the paper for every amateur food and flower grower. It offers free advice (in cases of urgency by 'phone) on all garden difficulties, and provides just the articles the amateur needs—simply explained, full of "specialist" hints, and illustrated by wonderful how-to-do-it photographs.

HOME GARDENING

EVERY **2**D. FRIDAY

Place a regular order with your Newsagent To-day

but that suited wartime conditions because gardeners had little time or space for difficult flowers. Sweet peas were a wartime favourite, and fitted well into the small space left for flowers growing among the vegetables. Carter's Seeds listed over seventy varieties, as well as 'Special Mixes' of different colour themes. 'Coronation', a selection 'of the finest variety from each of the red, white and blue sections in equal proportion', made a suitably patriotic statement. Unwins sold thirty-six sweet pea plants for 3s, ready hardened off, and described as 'The Ideal Flowers for War-Time Growing'. Asters also made what *Garden Work for Amateurs* described as 'A brave show', with blooms carried into the winter in a cool greenhouse – which all greenhouses were after the introduction of wartime fuel restrictions. Antirrhinums were ideal for squeezing into a spare corner, especially the popular Tom Thumb varieties. Colour contrasts, so popular in the 1930s, could be easily achieved with all colours available – from crimson, pink,

Annuals such as zinnia, verbena and nemesia were easy and quick to grow.

Russell lupins, named after the breeder George Russell, came in two tones, as well as every colour of the rainbow.

scarlet, yellow and salmon – and combinations with dual colours. Lupins, a perennial plant, came in startling colour combinations because of the 'Russell' lupin introduced in 1937, although few had reached suburban gardeners before the great 1939 'cut down'. Bright colours were also contributed by annuals such as nasturtiums, larkspurs, zinnias and marigolds.

Speed was a great advantage in a period when no one knew what the next few months would bring. Night-scented stock grew from seed to flower in as little as ten weeks, and dahlias were advertised as 'seed to flower in five months'. 'Quick growing climbers' such as nasturtiums were recommended by *Garden Work for Amateurs* for camouflaging Anderson shelters and ARP posts! Scabious were recommended for table decorations, along with zinnias and the useful 'everlasting flower' such as Helichrysum or statice. Nicotiana was sold both as the sweet-scented varieties and (also in the flower catalogue) as 'Mixed Smoking Tobacco' – a temptation for smokers who found it increasingly hard to get cigarettes in wartime.

Patriotism crept into the flower border as well as the vegetable bed. Dwarf godetias were described as 'Grand for the Front Line of beds and borders'; Allwoods' pinks could be bought in a 'Spitfire' collection, which included the varieties Blenheim, Sunderland, Hudson and Merlin, as well as Spitfire. Tulipland's Pedigree Bulbs provided a 'National Colour' collection of red, white and 'blue' tulips – ideal for flower borders where, the company warned, 'vegetables will not grow' because 'they would be eaten by caterpillars and give your home a miserable appearance'. The Home Guard potatoes, developed in 1942 for

Choosing a flower with an appropriate name gave some consolation to those gardeners plagued by concerns that planting flowers might be seen as unpatriotic.

their early cropping and consistent (although often moderate) yields, also gained popularity because of their name.

Advertisers also latched on to the patriotic wartime gardening mood. Chase Continuous Cloches used the memorable slogan 'Cloches versus Hitler' and offered purchasers a booklet of the same title, authored by the suspiciously named 'Charles Wyse-Gardner'. 'Victory Garden Certainty' came with insecticides sold by Corry & Co, Bakers Seeds produced 'Vegetables of National Importance' and Mortegg (Tar Wash) claimed 'Aphid Raid Protection [ARP]'. The unfortunately chosen 'Mortegg as Your Maginot Line'

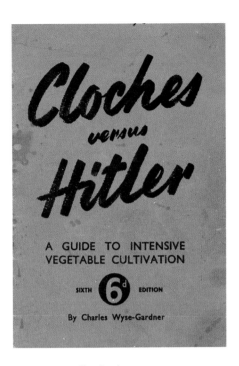

A GUIDE TO INTENSIVE VEGETABLE CULTIVATION

SIXTH 6d EDITION

By Charles Wyse-Gardner

advertisement ended as the real Maginot Line was outflanked by the German army in 1940. As digging for victory became entrenched in everyday life, other goods and services referred to it, however seemingly remote they were from the actual task of gardening. Soaps and beauty products were targeted at the newly gardening housewife, presumably concerned about the effect of digging on her appearance; whisky was sold with Dig for Victory booklets in the background – a drink as a reward for hard work done perhaps? Furniture polish made the task of housekeeping easier when the allotment awaited you, and Ferranti radios (should you have been lucky enough to buy one before the war) were advertised as ideal for listening to Cecil Middleton's *In Your Garden* on the Home Service.

Chase Continuous Cloches justified their advertising slogan by arguing that longer cropping seasons would mean success on the Home Front and help win the food war.

Seed suppliers struggled with labour shortages, shortages of paper (for packets and catalogues) and post sacks, as well as disrupted postage and carriage restrictions. In keeping with the Dig for Victory campaign, vegetable seed catalogues

Flower and vegetable seeds came in wartime economy packaging, giving little indication of the glories to be expected.

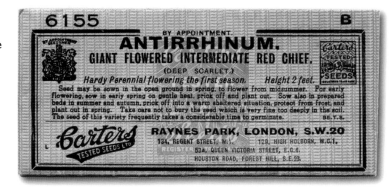

Dating from 1939, these cigarette cards include the most popular garden flowers of the period.

were free to obtain, but flower catalogues were charged for. In 1939 plant nurseries had been instructed to stop all planting of perennials or nursery stock only 75 per cent of 'under glass' areas were to be allowed for flowers and 50 per cent of any outdoor areas. By 1942 this had shrunk to 10 per cent of glasshouse area and 25 per cent of outside areas. In order to comply with the restriction, nurseries were forced to plough in or pull up precious stock. Between 1939 and 1944 land under flower and nursery stock fell nationally from 25,000 acres to 9,000 acres. Ironically, demand for flowers was high, with an increase in weddings and funerals, and seeing flower prices rise while being forced to plough in bulbs was especially difficult for nurseries struggling to

ASHTON BROTHERS AND CO. LIMITED

DIG FOR VICTORY

VEGETABLE AND FLOWER SHOW

SEPTEMBER 21ST, 1942 23 AUG 1943

SECOND PRIZE

CLASS No. 96

NAME S. Grime

(SIX ANTIRRHINHUMS)

Antirrhinums were a popular wartime flower. Note the reused flower show prize certificate and the slight misspelling.

survive. Woods Nursery in Woodbridge (Suffolk) converted five of their seven glasshouses to tomatoes, ousting their rare chrysanthemums created by Roger Crompton Notcutts, while Allwoods (Sussex), peacetime specialists in carnations and pinks, converted to production of peas and onions. In Devon, a nurseryman was fined £15 for growing tulips instead of vegetables.

Where flower growing did continue, it added an extra dimension to the popular Dig for Victory (or Victory Garden) shows that soon gained popularity across the country – often combined with Red Cross fetes or 'Warship Weeks', or even 'Fur and Feather' shows in more rural areas. The Red Cross Agricultural Fund was active in promoting 'Garden Weeks' and issued a leaflet on how to organise these extended events. The Royal Horticultural Society also held floral meetings and shows through much of the war, after a brief halt in 1939–40, although the challenges faced by contributors included not only growing the flowers but getting them to the meetings, as petrol was rationed and rail travel restricted. Better by far, the government announced, to stay at home and enjoy the garden!

THE COUNTRY-HOUSE GARDEN AT WAR

ALTHOUGH THE DIG for Victory campaign was primarily aimed at the working and middle classes, the government also had its keen eyes on the contribution that could be made by owners of large country houses and estates. At the declaration of war, many of these had received requisition notices and already housed everything from maternity hospitals and private schools to military units and even, at Ashton Wold (Northamptonshire), the British Museum Worm Collection (as well as a Red Cross unit, and an American airfield). These new occupants had to be fed, and the productive gardens were under pressure to perform. Unfortunately the very gardeners who would normally have coaxed the gardens to maximum productivity were subject to conscription, and their place was taken by young trainees, overseen by those too old to serve, or in ill-health. Initially conscription affected only those whose duties lay in the decorative gardens, and professional gardeners who could prove themselves engaged in food production were 'reserved', but for private estates the division was often unclear. In November 1941 the Minister of Agriculture announced that 'except in the largest of gardens it is expected that the owners and occupiers will themselves undertake the work of cultivating the ground without calling upon the assistance of able-bodied men eligible for national service'. *Ideal Home and Gardening* included a regular column by two women detailing their struggles in the garden after their gardener had been called up.

Country-house gardens could often provide enough food to support the men billeted there.

Abundant crops to swell the country's reserves should reward you if you listen to George E. Whitehead, F.R.H.S.

Large areas of glasshouses in country house kitchen gardens were converted to tomato production to help provide sources of vitamin C.

With increasing emphasis on food production, the Ministry finally responded to criticism of its wasteful deployment of skilled gardeners as infantrymen by instituting the 'soldier-gardener' scheme. The scheme identified trained gardeners within the forces and deployed them to make billeted units self-sufficient. In 1943 Southern Command troops alone produced 10,400 tons of vegetables from country-house gardens and smaller barrack plots under this scheme.

In return for a commitment to become a 'registered food production' site, supplying food either direct to troops or to the local population, a fuel allowance could be made for the glasshouses, which many a skilled head gardener then 'shared out' with his stock of rare flowering plants. At Nuneham Park (Oxfordshire) a crop of peaches was maintained, tucked in the shelter of tomato plants, while at Lulworth (Dorset) the tomatoes shared with vines – to the detriment of the tomatoes. At Ditchley Park (Oxfordshire) flowers still predominated, as dahlias and begonias were swapped for the easier-maintenance lavender and rosemary. The walled kitchen or 'productive' gardens of larger houses needed little or no structural adaptation for wartime production, but the crops were changed under the ever vigilant eyes of the War Agricultural Executive Committee county representatives. Commonly known as 'War Ags', they had the unenviable task of overseeing productivity of farms and large estates in their regions and, on a smaller scale, had powers to 'advise' head gardeners of country houses on the crops they should produce. Typically, glasshouse crops were converted from peaches and grapes to lettuces, carrots and tomatoes, and asparagus and strawberry beds were dug up for more 'practical' cabbages and brassicas.

Enrolment in the official food-production scheme might also bring the assistance of the Women's Land Army – as did the adaptation of walled gardens to become private market gardens – a fate suffered by many a private estate during and after the war years. At Aynhoe Park (Northamptonshire) the head gardener ran the kitchen and greenhouses as a market garden privately, after the army took over part of the house. The army proved both a blessing and a hindrance – purchasing his produce, especially rare peaches, nectarines, and grapes, but also felling fruit trees, camping on flower borders, and breaking into the greenhouses.

The Women's Land Army took over the walled gardens and parks of many country houses.

Walled gardens became centres of production, with produce often sold at the gate or shipped to nearby markets or military posts.

With kitchen gardens being kept in productivity, it was the decorative borders and bedding that suffered. In September 1939 the *Gardeners' Chronicle* (the choice of professional gardeners and country house owners) gave its first judgement on the impact of war on the country-house garden: 'All so-called luxury gardening will have to be curtailed for various reasons, such as lack of labour, fuel for glasshouses, taxation, and probably petrol; for motor-mowers etc., so economy will have to be practised and this can be accomplished in many ways ... Pleasure garden work, such as the mowing of lawns, will proceed normally this year, but next year it may have to be curtailed and probably only the lawns surrounding the house will be kept in order.' As the war progressed, many estates did not even have the house lawns mown, and bedding increasingly included vegetables that had decorative foliage, such as the carrots and beetroot at Blenheim Palace (Oxfordshire). At Longford Castle (Wiltshire) the Earl of Radnor converted the sunken Italian garden to the production of onions, while in the royal gardens at Sandringham (Norfolk) beetroot and parsnips filled the beds in the ornamental flower garden, and rye and oats were sown on the lawns and golf course. At Hampton Court Palace (Surrey) 120 acres of the park and gardens were given to vegetable cultivation. An East Anglian newspaper told its readers of a colonel home after four years in Burma, who asked his gardener how the lawns were looking. 'Well Sir', was the reply, 'you are having spuds off the tennis lawn tonight, and Cook tells me you are having a special salad from the croquet lawn.'

There were, however, some instances where the government, with advice from the Royal Horticultural

This advertisement for Green's Lawnmowers, dating to 1944, highlighted the struggles faced by owners of larger gardens and grounds in their attempts to keep up pre-war standards.

FLOWER BORDERS will grow excellent food crops. Here is a border with cabbages and brussels sprouts in front and a row of peas behind. In the garden of L. J. Hovey, Esq., at Beckenham. Carters.

Flower borders full of vegetables were the order of the day.

Opposite: Children evacuated to country houses as part of school or nursery moves often recall their time in the gardens there with pleasure.

Country houses in use as hospitals or recuperation centres often used the ornamental gardens as therapy, with some of the inmates helping with upkeep.

Society, felt that garden destruction was not in the nation's interest. At Leigh Park (Hampshire) the gardens were maintained to a high standard to disguise the estate's use as a navy training site, including testing of mines in the grounds. Levens Hall (Cumbria), famous for its ancient topiary, was allocated an extra petrol allowance to cut the yews once a year with petrol-driven hedge clippers. Other national collections, such as the Rothschild orchids, were given allowances for hothouse fuel. At the outbreak of war, there had even been a scheme suggested whereby gardeners might be retained for gardens of particular merit, although this, and other volunteer schemes, do not appear to have been taken up unless some element of productivity could be proven. On the thousands of country estates used for hospitals, or for rest and recuperation, the gardens were often kept up by the new inhabitants as part of their rehabilitation, and flowers played their part by 'brightening parks and gardens and bringing their cheerfulness into homes, hospitals and sickrooms' as the editor of the *Gardener's Chronicle* enthused.

RYDERS' FAMOUS COLLECTION

This well-tried collection is, and has been, a firm favourite with generations of gardeners. The varieties which we select are of proved garden merit and will provide fresh vegetables of excellent quality.

A packet of each of the following, containing the requisite quantity for an Allotment or Plot of 10 perches (about 300 square yards):

BEET, Globe, ½ oz.
FRENCH BEANS, ¼ pt.
RUNNER BEANS, ¼ pt.
BORECOLE (Kale), 4d. pkt.
BROCCOLI, 4d. pkt.
BRUSSELS SPROUTS,
    4d. pkt.
CABBAGE, Spring, 4d. pkt.
CABBAGE, Autumn, 4d. pkt.
SAVOY CABBAGE, 4d. pkt.
CARROT, Intermediate, ½ oz.
CRESS, 4d. pkt.
LETTUCE, Cabbage, 4d. pkt.
LETTUCE, Cos, 4d. pkt.

MUSTARD, 4d. pkt.
ONION, for Spring use,
    6d. pkt.
ONION, for Main Crop,
    6d. pkt.
PARSLEY, 4d. pkt.
PARSNIP, 4d. pkt.
PEAS, Early, ½ pt.
PEAS, Maincrop, ½ pt.
RADISH, 4d. pkt.
CAULIFLOWER, 6d. pkt.
TURNIP, 4d. pkt.
VEGETABLE MARROW,
    4d. pkt.

CARRIAGE
PAID **7/6**

RYDERS' 'COMPLETE GARDEN' COLLECTION

Offered in the National Press for the first time last season, this collection achieved immediate popularity and the demand far exceeded our expectations.

VEGETABLES

Complete Selection as offered above in Ryders' Famous 'V' Collection.

FLOWERS

Twelve generous fourpenny packets of popular annuals, our selection.

CARRIAGE
PAID **10/-**

It is possible for us to offer these collections at such advantageous prices, as they are assembled and packed in advance of the busiest period of our season. In the circumstances, no alterations can be made in the contents, but we can promise prompt despatch. These collections of high-quality seeds are normally sent by return.

Carriage Paid terms in respect of these collections apply in England, Scotland, Wales and N. Ireland.

DIG FOR PEACE,
DIG FOR PLENTY

As the longed-for peace became more of a future reality than a far-off dream, so the victory diggers of England started to pause in their efforts. By 1943, when Lord Woolton was rather optimistically appointed Minister of Reconstruction, many gardeners were impatient to abandon the vegetable plot and reconstruct their flower borders. In July 1942 Cecil Middleton and his listeners took it for granted that he would talk about 'leeks, lettuces, and leather-jackets', rather than 'lilac, lilies, and lavender', but in February 1944 – with VE Day still fifteen months away – he was forced to try and bring them back to the Dig for Victory fold. 'There is nothing', he said, 'I would like better than to put my lawn down again and to refurnish the borders; I should just love to cut bunches of roses and lilac and herbaceous flowers again, but the time is not yet. The need for growing food at home is as great, if not greater, than at any time during the war, and we must not relax for a moment, rather should we make still greater efforts for we may yet know what it is to be hungry.'

In 1944 a 'Gallup' poll by the British Institute of Public Opinion indicated that over 50 per cent of people assumed that once peace was declared rationing would ease and food supplies would flow in from pre-war supply lines again. Allotment take-up began to slump, and in response the government, headed by the Ministry of Agriculture and Ministry of Information, launched new advertising campaigns. At the opening of every Dig for Victory show in the summer of 1944 a telegram from

The transition between war and peace was to be a prolonged one. This early 1950s advertisement for Ryders' seeds still gave prominence to vegetables over flowers.

'Dig On for Victory', 'Dig for Plenty' and 'Dig for Peace' were all phrases used in the final year of the war.

the Minister of Agriculture was read out to further encourage efforts: 'We have, in the last five years, achieved on the garden and allotment fronts a great deal of which we can be proud. But the war is not yet won, and even when the Nazi gangsters are beaten, food will be scarce. Perhaps scarcer than now. So carry on – do not rest on your spades, except for those brief periods which are every gardener's privilege.' New slogans and new posters were tried out, including 'Dig On for Victory', 'Dig to Keep Well Fed' and 'The need is GROWING'. A short campaign saw 'old hands' encouraged to provide advice and encouragement to new diggers, and planning for the future was the new theme. 'You Need A Plan' and 'Better Planning, Better Gardening, Better Crops' sparked applications for the constantly reissued *Planning a Plot* Dig for Victory leaflets. For those who still did not have access to an allotment, Dig for Victory Leaflet No. 24 was on the subject of *Roof and Window-box Gardening*, and the Ministry of Agriculture's warning that 'we shall have to maintain Home Food Production to the utmost into the post-war years' might have encouraged windows everywhere to be decorated with lettuces.

The removal of park railings in Britain (for their metal content) had brought into sharp focus the worth of humble vegetables, as they became increasingly subject to theft. Stealing from wartime vegetable gardens was classed as 'looting', and could result in a heavy fine or even a prison term. Onions were the most common casualties of theft as they have to be left on the surface to dry out once harvested, but leeks and other above-ground vegetables suffered as rationing became tighter.

If the situation was difficult in Britain, it was worse in much of occupied Europe. By the end of 1945 the scheme of allotments and home food producers was in use across mainland Europe to try to stave off a humanitarian disaster. In Germany food rations had been severely cut since the winter of 1944, and, with the collapse of the Nazi regime and the destruction of transport links, the winter of 1946–7 was to become known as the 'Hunger Winter'. The Royal Horticultural Society sent its popular image-based *The Vegetable Garden Displayed* into Germany but by the spring of 1946 it was estimated that calorific provision in the British-occupied zone fell as low as 1,050 calories a day. In Moscow, over 1.5 million people turned 35,000 acres into allotments and Victory Gardens, while across the Soviet Union as a whole 11.5 million people cultivated plots.

One of the last Dig for Victory leaflets to be issued appealed to those who really did not have any garden space!

Commencing in January 1945, the year that was finally to see both victory in Europe and victory over Japan, the government brought out its own monthly *Allotment & Garden Guides*. The guides eschewed such fripperies as flowers and concentrated on 'helping you get better results from your vegetable plot and fruit garden'. Providing an overview of what needed doing that month, what should have been done the previous month, and the ideal of planning ahead for the next month, the guides carried the unwelcome message that 'this will be the tightest of the war years so far as food supplies are concerned' and that only those who did not 'rest on their spades' would be able to provide for their families. As demobilsation started, and rationing tightened (with bread being rationed for the first time from July 1946), the 1943 prophecy by Robert Hudson (Minister for Agriculture) that 'When the day of victory dawns the need for the little man and his wife to go on producing their own food will be just as pressing' was fulfilled.

With the end of the war, public parks and private land that had been requisitioned for the provision of allotments were returned to their original purposes, often with only a few months warning for the irate allotment holders. Allotment numbers fell rapidly from 1.5 million to around 500,000 in the following decades. After the First World War an almost immediate decline in allotment numbers had conflicted with increased demand by returning servicemen facing economic depression, but after five years of war on the Garden Front many allotment holders had had enough by 1946. In an attempt to keep up interest even the *Allotment & Garden Guides* had to admit that a 'happy fringe of flowers' around the edge of an allotment was allowable, although any more than 10 per cent of a plot devoted to flowers on a plot merited an inquisition by the local allotment association.

Allotment & Garden Guides were published every month through 1945. The request to 'Please Keep' hinted not only at economy but that they would be needed in future years.

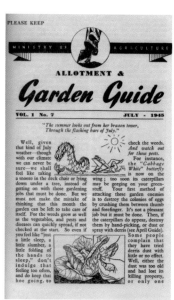

The winter of 1946–7 was one of the worst on record, with large swathes of the country enveloped in fog and snow from 21 January to 16 March 1947. Root vegetables were impossible to extract from frozen ground, and even winter cabbage, leeks and Brussels sprouts suffered under the extreme conditions. For the plant nurseries battling to recover from the wartime restrictions this was a final blow. Plants that had survived the war suffered in the freeze, and many businesses were forced to rebuild their stock from European and American nurseries. In 1948 the charismatic Harry Wheatcroft imported a peachy-yellow standard rose that was to repopulate the gardens of the post-war suburbs; he called it 'Peace'.

EPILOGUE

In his 1940 book *War-Time Gardening*, John Reed Wade referred to the 'great and magnificent effort for victory on the home front' that lay within the hands of all those who owned a garden, and throughout the war years statistics released to the press emphasised the contribution made by gardeners to the 'Food Front'. In July 1943 the Minister of Agriculture informed the House of Commons that the Dig for Victory campaign had made an 'invaluable contribution' to making families self-supporting, with allotment numbers rising from 930,000 in 1939 to 1,675,000 at the current date. The number of private gardens growing vegetables had also, he said, risen from three million to five million (rather incredibly, given that there were only an estimated 3.5 million private gardens at the start of the war) and *The Times* went as far as to declare that an area as large as the county of Huntingdonshire was currently under cultivation. In the 1942–3 season, one gardening periodical estimated that 1,000,000 tons of vegetables had been produced on allotments, and in December 1944 the *Gardeners' Chronicle* computed the annual vegetable contribution of each allotment holder as equivalent to £10 a plot, going on to confidently surmise that £17,250,000 was therefore the total value of food produced by allotmenters during the war years.

There was, however, another version of these enthusiastically optimistic figures. In the late summer of 1942 a survey by the government found that only 50 per cent of urban households were growing their own vegetables, with figures as low as

'Food Fights for Freedom' as Winston Churchill backed the final year of the Dig for Victory campaign.

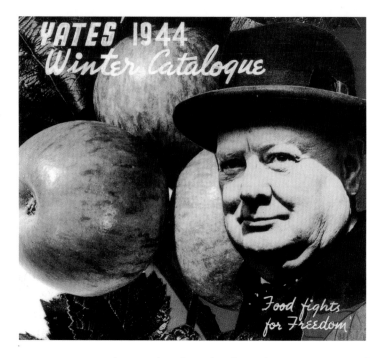

39 per cent in the north of England. Only 16 per cent of allotmenters surveyed had taken on an allotment as a result of the Dig for Victory campaign materials, and only 4.5 per cent of these were growing the vital winter brassicas so heavily promoted. By June 1944 the overall figures were lower, with only 34 per cent of urban households growing vegetables in their gardens, and 10 per cent cultivating an allotment. In the north-west three-quarters of all households failed to grow any foodstuffs at all, a figure similar to the hub of the campaign in inner London. Almost all surveys failed to take into account country dwellers, who were merely assumed to be growing their own food, mainly because they always had.

Whether in reality the wartime populace enthusiastically dug for victory, or merely fell asleep to the soporific tones of Mr Middleton, the wartime garden rapidly took on the mythical quality of a shared past: a Garden Front where beans battled bullets and cloches stood firm against Hitler.

FURTHER READING

Brown, Mike. *Wartime Britain*. Shire Living Histories, 2011.

Brown, Mike, and Harris, Carol. *The Wartime House: Life in Wartime Britain 1939–45*. Sutton Publishing, 2001.

Buchan, Ursula. *A Green and Pleasant Land: How England's Gardeners Fought the Second World War*. Hutchinson, 2013.

Davies, Jennifer. *The Wartime Kitchen and Garden*. BBC Books, 1993.

Middleton, Cecil. *Digging for Victory: Wartime Gardening with Mr Middleton*. Aurum Press, 2008 (reprint of wartime radio talks).

Seebohm, Caroline. *The Country House: A Wartime History 1939–45*. Weidenfeld & Nicolson, 1989.

Smith, Daniel. *The Spade as Mighty as the Sword: The Story of World War Two's Dig for Victory Campaign*. Aurum Press, 2011.

Way, Twigs. *Allotment & Garden Guide: A Monthly Guide to Better Wartime Gardening*. Sabrestorm Publishing, 2009 (facsimiles of 1945 garden guides with commentary).

Way, Twigs. *A Nation of Gardeners: How the British Fell in Love with Gardening*. Prion Books, 2010.

Way, Twigs and Brown, Mike. *Digging for Victory: Gardens and Gardening in Wartime Britain*. Sabrestorm Publishing, 2010 (heavily illustrated).

WEBSITES

BBC archive of people's Second World War memories:
www.bbc.co.uk/history/ww2peopleswar
Pathé News Online: www.britishpathe.com
Imperial War Museum: www.iwm.org.uk

INDEX